P9-CQW-574
3 4863 00473 1411

WITHDRAWN

GIANT STONES AND EARTH MOUNDS

GIANT STONES AND EARTH MOUNDS

Tom McGowen

The Millbrook Press
Brookfield, Connecticut

Cover photograph courtesy of Photo Researchers, Inc. (© Fred Espenak/SPL)

Photographs courtesy of Woodfin Camp & Associates: pp. 8 (© Adam Woolfitt), 26 (© Anthony Marshal, DTM); Brian Hope Taylor/NGS Image Collection: p. 12; The Image Works: pp. 18 (© Macduff Everton), 20 (© Lee Snider); Corbis: pp. 17 (© Chris Taylor; Cordaiy Photo Library Ltd.), 22 (© Gianni Dagli Orti), 31 (© Richard A. Cooke), 62 (© Adam Woolfitt), 63 (© Kevin Schafer), 67 (© Adam Woolfitt); Photo Researchers, Inc.: pp. 25 (© Fred Espenak/SPL), 47 (© Lawrence Migdale); © Tom Till: p. 32; © Diego Meozzi: pp. 34, 37, 54; Tony Stone Images: p. 39 (© Joe Cornish); © C. M. Dixon: p 40; © University of Colorado at Boulder/Ken Abbott: p. 44; © English Heritage Photographic Library: pp. 51, 57, 69, 72; Britstock: p. 65 (© 1993 Ronald Gorbutt)

Library of Congress Cataloging-in-Publication Data
McGowen, Tom.
Giant stones and earth mounds / by Tom McGowen.
p. cm.
Includes bibliographical references and index.
Summary: Describes the mysterious standing stones and earth mounds which were built by Stone Age peoples and explores how and why they may have been built.
ISBN 0-7613-1372-9 (lib. bdg.)
1. Megalithic monuments—Juvenile literature. 2. Mounds—Juvenile literature. 3. Neolithic period—Juvenile literature. [1. Megalithic monuments. 2. Mounds.] I. Title.
GN790.M39 2000
930.1'4—dc21 00-025687

Published by The Millbrook Press, Inc.
2 Old New Milford Road
Brookfield, Connecticut 06804
www.millbrookpress.com

Printed in the United States of America
5 4 3 2 1

CONTENTS

GIANT STONES AND EARTH MOUNDS

The Ring of Brogar in the Orkneys, Scotland

1
THE NEW STONE AGE: MEGALITHS, MOUNDS, AND MYSTERY

Throughout the world, sometimes within the heart of busy, modern communities, there stand huge, mysterious remains of another world that existed thousands of years ago—the dim, remote, prehistoric time called the New Stone Age.

The New Stone Age came at the end of the vast period of some two million years known overall as the Stone Age. It was given that name by scientist John Lubbock in the mid-nineteenth century because humans all over the world made most of their tools and weapons from stone during those millions of years. Metal was unknown.

Scientists divide the Stone Age into three periods—Old Stone Age, Middle Stone Age, and New Stone Age. The Old Stone Age was a long period of time, during which primitive humans gradually became more like the people of today. Humans who looked just like us began to appear in the world about 40,000 years ago. These people were nomadic hunters, who followed the herds of deer and other creatures that were their main source of food. They killed their prey with spears tipped with points of chipped stone. But as thousands of years passed, their weapons and tools improved. They learned to grow plants as their major source of food, to tame animals and form herds of livestock, to make pots and containers out of baked clay, and to live in settled communities instead of always moving about. This marked the beginning of the New Stone Age.

The World's First Buildings

The New Stone Age came at different times in different parts of the world—about 9,000 years ago in the Middle East, 7,000 years ago in Europe, 3,500 years ago in America. But when people reached this point they began to build things other than just huts to live in. Stone was the hardest, longest-lasting material they knew of, and earth was a plentiful substance that could be piled up in huge quantities. So they used stone and earth to create great imposing structures that were the world's first buildings.

The New Stone Age ended thousands of years ago, when people learned how to produce metal, but many of the structures built then have lasted to this day. Western Europe, and particularly the islands of Britain and Ireland, abound with them, but they are also found in many other parts of the world. Most of them were built with gigantic boulders, which scientists have given the name *megaliths*, from two Greek words meaning "great stone." They are also sometimes called *menhirs*, from two old French words meaning "long stone." Some structures are rings and rows of huge upright megaliths. Some are tunnels and chambers of piled stones covered with long mounds of earth. Some are dome-shaped earthen mounds as big as hills. Some are great circular walls of earth. Some are simply enormous, heavy megaliths that were set up to stand all by themselves, like lonely sentinels or guardians.

Many Questions

Around our world, we have remnants of the New Stone Age, standing like great, imposing monuments. But there is a mystery about most of these things—it must have been tremendously diffi-

Tales From the New Stone Age?

Throughout the parts of Europe where New Stone Age people built mounds and megalithic structures, there are many ancient legends of strange things.

One of the most common is of tiny humanlike creatures that live underground and guard the earth's treasures. They are known as Dwarfs, in Britain; Svart Alfar, in the Norse countries; Gnomes, in France; and Kobolds, in Germany. It was said they sometimes took human miners captive, or attacked them with cave-ins.

Another common legend is of creatures that were guardians of forests. In what is now Finland, this creature was known as Tapio; in Russia and other eastern lands it was called the Leshy; in Germany it was the Wildenmann; and in Britain, the Green Man. These forest guardians were believed to be able to magically cause humans to get lost in the woods.

Most common of all, everywhere, were legends of the dragons—gigantic fire-breathing, flying reptiles that sometimes demanded the sacrifice of young girls to keep from destroying human farms and communities.

There is no way of telling just how old most of these legends are. Could some of them have their beginnings in the time of the New Stone Age, or earlier? Vast forests covered much of the land in Stone Age times, and Stone Age people, digging for the stone called flint, were probably the world's first miners. Could these tales of forest guardians, underground dwellers, and dragons have come from the New Stone Age? If so, they show us the kind of world that New Stone Age people believed they lived in—a world of magical beings and supernatural terrors!

Moving the stones and shaping the earth for the New Stone Age monuments were remarkable feats, accomplished for some great reason. But the reasons are still to be learned.

cult for prehistoric people, with no machinery and no beasts of burden, to build these huge structures. Most of them were built by the efforts of many people over many years, often over many centuries. Obviously, they were tremendously important to the people who made them. But the question is, why were they so important? Why would people labor for years to build a circle of gigantic stones or a huge artificial hill of earth? What were they for? What did they mean to the people who made them?

Still another puzzle is how and why many of these prehistoric structures were changed over the course of many centuries, by different groups of New Stone Age people. The famous stone circle Stonehenge, in England, was changed several times over a 2,000-year period. Things were taken out of it, and things were added to it. Why? About 1,000 years after the great passage-grave mound of Newgrange was built in Ireland, a circle of about 35 huge standing stones was erected around it. Why?

DIFFERENT PEOPLE, DIFFERENT WAYS OF THOUGHT

We know a great deal about the New Stone Age people who built these kinds of structures in Europe. They were generally smaller than we are, the biggest of them about 5 feet 6 inches (1.6 m) tall. They wore clothing made of animal hides, bark cloth, and woven dried grass. Examinations of their skeletons show that they suffered from many diseases and health problems. Probably half of all their children died before reaching the age of three, and about four out of every ten grown-ups died before they reached the age of twenty. Many died in their thirties, and forty was about as old as most of them got.

We can be sure that these people did not think about things as we do. They were just as intelligent, but they simply did not know all the things we know, and this would have caused them to think about the world differently from the way we do. They did not know what the sun was, or the moon, or the stars. They did not know why there was night and day, or why summer and winter occurred. They did not know what caused diseases. And so they lived in a world full of mysteries and uncertainties, which probably made them

A Man of the New Stone Age

We have more than just skeletons and stone implements to help us know about Stone Age people and their way of life. Amazing though it seems, the body of a New Stone Age man, with his clothing, weapons, and personal possessions, was discovered in 1991 in the Alps of Italy. The man had apparently been caught in a sudden blizzard and crawled into a crevice in the rocks, where he froze to death. His body became covered with ice and was buried beneath a glacier, which kept his skin and flesh, as well as the wood and leather of his clothing and possessions, frozen and preserved for 5,300 years!

The man's belongings showed that New Stone Age people were capable of producing such things as well-made leather tunics, leggings, moccasin-like shoes, fur caps, and capes made of braided dried grass. The man carried a wooden bow and stone-tipped arrows in a leather quiver, and an ax with a copper head mounted on a wooden handle. In a fur bag were tools made of stone and bone, for cutting and slicing things, for making holes in leather, and for sewing. He also had a piece of flint and a chunk of iron ore, which when struck together would produce sparks that could kindle a fire.

People like this man built the great mounds and megalithic structures that stand throughout Europe.

fearful. When summer came to an end, they could never be sure that there would ever be another summer—perhaps the winter would last forever. An event such as an eclipse of the sun, or the appearance of a comet, filled them with terror. And their way of thinking about their world and its mysteries and terrors may explain why they built the kinds of structures they did.

The Modern World's Puzzles From the Past

Because we really can't get into the minds of people with such a different way of thinking, and such a different way of life, we can't be sure why they built those great earth mounds and circles of giant stones and other structures. Most of those people never invented any form of writing, so they couldn't pass on any explanation of why they built the things they did. Thus it is left to us today to try to figure out the reasons for the giant prehistoric structures that still stand as puzzles throughout the world. Were they tombs? Were they temples of long-forgotten religions? Were they monuments of some sort? Were they, as some astronomers believe, a way of measuring the movement of the sun, moon, and constellations? Why were some of them changed after hundreds and even thousands of years? Were they changed to make them better? Were they changed to turn them into something else?

No one really knows any of the answers for sure. Prehistoric people of the New Stone Age, who were the ancestors of many people living now, left behind these imposing works of stone and earth, and scientists of today are striving to learn what those structures may have meant. A few things have been discovered about them—some surprising, some disturbing—but most are still cloaked in mystery.

2

EARTH MOUNDS, STONE TABLES, AND ARTIFICIAL HILLS

In the open countryside in many parts of western Europe stand long grass-covered swellings of earth, sometimes with trees growing on them. They are known in English by the names *mound*, *barrow*, or *tumulus*. There is a smoothness and a shape to these mounds that reveals they are not simply ordinary hills. There are the remains of ditches around them, and it is obvious that the earth that forms the mounds must have come out of the ditches. The fact is, these mounds were *made*. They are some of the oldest human-made structures in the world. They were built by prehistoric people of the New Stone Age, as much as 7,000 years ago, and more.

Since that time, legends have become attached to these long mounds. Some of them are said to be homes of the Little People—the supernatural creatures of fairy tales. Some are said to be haunted. Some, it is claimed, are magical. But aside from the legends, there are real mysteries about these mounds.

The Making of the Mounds

The people who made the mounds used deer antlers to gouge soft rocks and chunks of turf out of the ground, and used the shoulder bones of cows, which have a natural shovel-shape, to dig up masses

West Kennet Long Barrow

An average mound is about 50 yards (45 m) long, 20 yards (18 m) wide, and 6 feet (2 m) high, but some are far bigger. A 5,250-year-old mound in England, known as the West Kennet Long Barrow, is 110 yards (100 m) long, 25 yards (22.5 m) wide at one end, and about 16 yards (14 m) at the other. From a distance, it looks like a huge snake stretched out on the ground, with a big head at one end and a tapering pointed tail at the other. Inside it is a long passageway formed of huge stones, with two small rooms coming off one side and three off the other.

The interior of West Kennet Long Barrow

of earth. The rocks and earth were then piled up to form the mounds. In places where there are many stones but not much dirt, the mounds were made of piled-up stones instead of earth.

Some of the mounds, generally the oldest ones, are solid earth throughout. But many had little rooms or chambers in them, made of logs or big stones. The stone chambers in many long mounds consisted of three or more huge rocks set upright in a cluster, with an immense boulder lying on top of them, like a roof. Because these structures look somewhat like huge tables, they are generally known as *dolmens*, from two Celtic words that mean "stone table." There are more than 15,000 dolmens in Europe, and thousands more scattered throughout much of the rest of the world. Some of them are buried or half-buried under mounds; many are standing

The Pentre Ifan burial chamber in Presely Hills, Wales, is a spectacular dolmen. The stones for Stonehenge might have been quarried nearby.

out in the open. (This is another mystery. Were those dolmens once inside mounds that have simply worn away, or were they always out in the open?)

Scientists have calculated that it would have taken at least ten people working every day for three months to construct even one of the average solid mounds. As for the dolmens, some of the stones forming these structures weigh more than 50 tons (45 metric tons), and it is amazing that prehistoric people, who had no machines for lifting and moving things, could have managed to bring such gigantic stones together in one place and pile them up in such a way. These were just ordinary people, for there were no such special workers as engineers or construction workers in prehistoric times. Obviously, the mounds must have been of great importance to those people, who were willing to work so long and hard to build them. What were they for?

Tombs for the Dead

For one thing, dead people were buried in them. The very oldest mounds, at least 7,000 years old, each contained the skeleton of one person, who was generally buried in a shallow grave that was then covered by the long high mound of earth. Most of these mounds are found in western Europe, from Poland to the British Isles.

Other mounds, not quite as old, contained the remains of many people—piles of human bones, of anywhere from a half-dozen to as many as several hundred persons. Some of these bone piles were buried at the bottoms of mounds that had been built over them, but others were piled up inside log chambers or dolmens within the mounds.

These mounds may well have been tombs for the dead. At first, perhaps only special people, such as chieftains or priests, had the honor of having a mound built over their graves. Then, as centuries went by, it apparently became the custom for everyone in a community to be buried in a mound.

But perhaps such mounds were actually more than just plain tombs. It is known that the bodies of people who died in those days

These burial mounds in County Meath, Ireland, were built circa 2500 B.C.

were not buried in the mounds at once; they were kept somewhere else until all the flesh had rotted off their bones. Sometimes, the bodies were burned, to get rid of the flesh quickly. Then the bones were taken to a mound and simply added to the pile that was there. But the piles of bones, whether they were in bare earth or in a chamber, were always at the east end of the mound, the end that faced the sunrise. The rest of the mound was left empty. Thus, it seems that the sun was considered important to the remains of the dead people in these mounds. There is evidence that there were sometimes meetings or ceremonies held by groups of people at the east ends of many mounds. So perhaps the mounds were more like shrines, or even temples, that was an important part of a religion that linked dead people with the sunrise.

Strange Legends of the Mounds

Legends connected with certain mounds seem to show that special sunrises were very important. In one legend about a mound in South Wales, in Britain, anyone who sleeps near the mound on the night before the sunrise of the first day of winter or the first day of summer (called Midwinter Day and Midsummer Day in Britain) will either be struck dead, go crazy—or become a poet! A legend about the West Kennet Long Barrow warns that on the night before the Midsummer Day sunrise, the mound is haunted by the ghost of an ancient priest and a huge white dog. Could such legends be memories of an ancient time when a mound was a holy place, and the first day of winter and summer were holy days, their sunrises and sunsets special events?

The Meaning of the Legend of Newgrange

For thousands of years, the big mound in Ireland called Newgrange lay in silent darkness, with its entrance closed. But there was a legend about it: that something strange happened *inside* Newgrange every year on December 21, the first day of winter. At sunrise on that day, it was said, the noiseless, lightless tomb became filled with light.

NEWGRANGE

There is no doubt that the great dome-shaped mound called Newgrange, in Ireland, had something to do with both death and a sunrise. Newgrange, like the West Kennet Long Barrow, is what is called a passage-grave—a tomb with a long hallway, or passage, running into it from an entrance. Constructed about 5,250 years ago, it is about 33 feet (10 m) high and 264 feet (80 m) wide. Some 200,000 softball-size white stones were pressed into the earth forming its base, so that it looks like a vast white wall with a dome-shaped green roof. Within it is a narrow 62-foot (19-m)-long passage, lined with slabs of stone. This leads into

a stone chamber that contained human bones and a small amount of ashes of burned human bones. Around Newgrange was a circle of approximately 35 huge megaliths, of which only 12 now stand, but this circle was put up 1,000 years after Newgrange was built.

In 1962 an Irish archaeologist, Michael O'Kelly, began to dig at Newgrange and opened it up. He discovered that there was a kind of small window just above the entrance, and in 1969, on a hunch, he went into the tomb on the morning of Midwinter Day, before sunrise, and waited. When the sun rose, a shaft of sunlight suddenly blazed through the window, flashed down the passageway, and lit up the entire inside of the tomb. The legend was true!

The little window is lined up with the point on the horizon where, each year on Midwinter Day, the sun rises. O'Kelly found evidence that the window was probably covered up all the rest of the year. Obviously, the people who built Newgrange planned very carefully to have the mound filled with sunlight for a few minutes on this one day of the year. There is evidence that the prehistoric name for Newgrange might have been "Cave of the Sun." Here, again, there seems to be a connection between the dead and the sunrise—a special, once-a-year sunrise.

A Religion of Sun-Worship

Experts think this may have had something to do with the religion of the New Stone Age people. Those people were farmers and herders, and their lives depended on the sprouting of seeds in the springtime and a summer of sunshine with enough rain to help the plants grow and provide a plentiful autumn harvest for them and their animals. They probably developed "magic" and a religion that would have seemed to them to be helpful in making these things happen. They could see that it was during the bright, sunny days of summer that plants grew, so they might have worshiped a god of the sun or perhaps the sun itself. At the beginning of spring, they might have held ceremonies and magical rituals that they hoped would bring the sunshine and rain that were needed to produce a good harvest. In winter, they could see that the sun seemed lower in the sky, and dimmer, and the days—the periods of sunlight—were shorter, and plants did not grow. So they might have held wintertime ceremonies and rituals, to help make the sun stronger again, and bring winter to an end.

The days on which they held such ceremonies were undoubtedly special to them. Throughout the northern part of the world one such day must surely have been December 21, Midwinter Day. Stone Age people must have been aware that the days leading up to Midwinter Day have shorter and shorter daylight periods until, finally, Midwinter Day has the shortest daylight period of all. But after that day, the daylight periods begin getting longer, foretelling the sure coming of spring. Another special day must have been the first day of May, called May Day, which has been celebrated for thousands of years in many northern parts of the world as the actual beginning of spring. So days such as May Day and Midwinter Day would have been very significant as days for special ceremonies.

The Sky Calendar

However, the people of the New Stone Age did not have such things as calendars. How could they know when these special days would be each year?

They knew by watching the sky.

Those people lived most of their lives out in the open, often out-of-doors both day and night. For them, sunrises and sunsets were not hidden by clustered houses or tall buildings. No blazing city lights or smoke-filled, polluted air masked out most of the stars. The Stone Age people could watch the movement of the sun, moon, and constellations, and see that the sun and moon rose and set on a different part of the horizon each day, and that different constellations appeared in the sky at certain seasons and vanished from the sky in others. Thus the sky became a calendar for them.

By noting the place on the horizon where the sun rose on a certain day, and by then setting up markers—wooden posts, piles of stones, or special big stones—that lined up exactly with the place where the sun rose, they created a way of measuring a year, the time between the day when the sun rose at that point and the day when it rose there again, some 365 days later. By watching from the markers, they could see the sun moving toward the point marked on the horizon, and know when to go each year to see the sunrise that meant the special day had dawned. They could use this way of

Prehistoric sites, such as Stonehenge, may have served as a calendar and a focus for ceremonies involving the seasons and stars and planets.

SILBURY HILL

Some of the mounds made by prehistoric people were huge, artificial hills. The largest artificial hill in Europe lies on a rolling plain in southern England. A cone-shaped, flat-topped mound known as Silbury Hill, the human-made hill is 132 feet (40 m) high and 544 feet (165 m) across at the base. Archaeologists have determined that it was built about 4,750 years ago, and legend says that it is the tomb of a great prehistoric chieftain, whose name was Sil, and who was buried wearing golden armor and sitting on a horse. But when archaeologists dug into it, no grave or any skeletons were found. So it does not seem to be a tomb at all. But if it is not a tomb, what was it for? What did this enormous artificial hill mean to the people who lived then?

marking sunrises or sunsets to keep track of many special days throughout the year.

The Origin of Months

While the sun was used as a calendar for measuring the length of a year, the moon became a way of measuring the periods of time within a year that we call months. Our word month comes from the old word *moonth*, which meant the period of time from when the first tiny curved sliver of the moon appeared to when the last tiny sliver vanished. Special moonrises could be marked just as sunrises and sunsets were, by lining up markers with the point where the moon first came up over the horizon. A certain moonrise in a certain *moonth* could mark the best day for starting to plant seeds, or the best day to begin harvesting. The rising of a star or constellation could also mark a special day.

Those places for watching special risings and settings of the sun, moon, stars, and constellations must have been extremely important to the people who used them. In time, they probably became holy or sacred places that were centers of religion, worship, and magic. It's in the nature of people to try to make such places seem grand and imposing, and it seems likely that the New Stone Age people did this.

Newgrange and many other mounds may have been built at just such places, where careful track could be kept of the sunrise of Midwinter Day and other sunrises. Letting the light of the Midwinter sunrise into Newgrange and holding sunrise ceremonies at other mounds might have had a deep religious meaning.

Of course, we can only guess at this. However, the inside of Newgrange is richly decorated, with many of the large stones forming its walls carved with swirling circular designs. This is true of other prehistoric passage-graves, such as the one known as Gavrinis, in France.

It seems obvious that the New Stone Age people wanted these places to be beautiful. Perhaps the passage-grave mounds were like cathedrals for them.

Mounds That Hint of Murder

Some of the mounds made by prehistoric people were huge artificial hills. A 7,000-year-old mound in France, the Tumulus of St. Michel, is big enough so that a chapel has been built on top of it.

Skeletons found in many of the mounds show that, aside from disease, many of these people apparently died from violence. The skulls of many of the skeletons were split, as if the people had been killed by blows to the head with a sharp weapon such as an ax. The skeleton of a 12- or 13-year-old boy, found in a 6,200-year-old mound in Denmark, revealed that the boy had been killed by an arrow shot into his chest. Were these people murdered by enemies, or perhaps killed in prehistoric battles? We know that these people did fight battles. The remains of a New Stone Age house were found that dramatically proves this. More than 200 arrows had been shot into it, by attackers who finally captured it and burned it to the ground.

Hints of Human Sacrifice

Of course, it is also possible that some of these people with split skulls were perhaps deliberately killed as sacrifices, to provide some kind of magical or protective power to the mound. There is not much doubt that such sacrifices did take place. A British archaeologist once made a careful examination of evidence found at a mound formed of piled-up stones in Wales, and pieced together a rather horrifying story. At the very bottom of the mound were the bones of a little girl. She had been killed, her body burned, and the bones put into a pit. Then a container filled with the ashes of a man's burned body had been placed on top of her bones. Trampled earth showed that many people had then danced around the bones and ashes. At a spot outside the ring of dancers, facing toward the setting sun, charcoal and plant ashes showed that a fire had been made and sheaves of wheat and barley from an autumn harvest had been thrown into it. It looks as if all this was a magical, religious ceremony—a sacrifice, the burial of some important person, a dance, an offering of the autumn harvest burned in flames. The people who did this probably believed they were making magic that would bring them good harvests in future years.

A Mound Mystery: The Case of the Missing Bones

Not only is the reason why prehistoric people built the great earth mounds a mystery, but there are often mysteries about things *in* the mounds as well.

In the long mound called West Kennet, in England, were piled the bones of forty-six people—men, women, and children. Most archaeologists believe that these people were all members of a nearby community, and probably all members of the same extended family. The bones are most likely the remains of many generations of the family.

Many of the bones had been carefully stacked against the walls of the stone chambers inside the mound, and others were piled on the floor. Archaeologists were able to put most of the bones together to form skeletons. But they found that a number of the skulls or jawbones of skulls were missing. And that is the mystery. Why were the entire skeletons of some people not buried? What was done with these parts of the skeletons?

Is it possible that these skulls and jawbones might have been kept by family members as mementos of beloved parents or favorite relatives? Perhaps they were kept in people's homes instead of being buried. Perhaps they were used for special ceremonies in some way. We don't know, and probably never shall.

Whether they were tombs or temples, many of the long mounds of Europe were used by people of the New Stone Age for many centuries, some as much as 2,000 years. Then, one by one, they were sealed up and no bones were ever put in them again. At the West

Kennet Long Barrow, about 4,200 years ago, each of the five bone-filled rooms was stuffed up with stones, bits of chalk, broken clay pottery, and animal bones. The whole passageway was filled with such things, and the area around the entrance was piled up with big rocks and then blocked off with three huge megaliths. Other mounds were sealed up in similar ways. The reason for this is another mystery—but it is almost as if the people sealing up these mounds were trying to make sure that the "spirits" of the dead inside could never possibly get out.

THE EARTH MOUNDS OF AMERICA

There are mounds in the United States much like some of those in Europe. They were made by several different groups of Native American people who lived from about 2,700 to nearly 300 years ago, in what are now the midwestern and southern United States. Even though the Stone Age was long over in Europe, these Native Americans were New Stone Age people, very much like those of Europe had been. They made good tools and weapons of stone, were skillful pottery makers, and knew how to farm. And like the prehistoric people of Europe, they buried the remains of their dead

MONKS MOUND

The largest American mound is not a tomb. Like Silbury Hill, in England, it is an artificial hill known today as Monks Mound (because a community of Catholic monks once lived on it), which stands near the town of Cahokia, in Illinois. Monks Mound is an enormous long mound, 100 feet (30 m) high, 710 feet (73 m) wide, and 1,080 feet (324 m) long. Its gigantic base is far bigger than that of the Great Pyramid of Egypt. But, like Silbury Hill there is nothing inside it, except a layer of

pebbles. No one was ever buried in it. What, then, was the purpose of this huge structure that must have taken years to build?

There were Native American people living in the Cahokia region when European explorers and settlers arrived there, and they told the newcomers what the mound had been for. It had been built to be the highest place in the region, and thus the closest place to the sun. It was made so that, every day, the chieftain who ruled the area—who was known as the "Brother of the Sun"—could stand on its top and greet the sun as it rose each morning. Of course, this was an act of worship, so the Cahokia mound must have been a holy place for the people of the region. Was Silbury Hill, in England, used in a similar way?

There are grave mounds at Cahokia, at least one of which hints at human sacrifice. The skeleton of a man found in it had been buried wearing a garment covered with beads made of snail shells, indicating that he may have been a chieftain. Buried with him were the skeletons of four young men and 53 women. Were these wives and warriors who had been sacrificed to serve the chieftain in an afterlife?

in big mounds of earth. One of the largest of these, the Grave Creek Mound in West Virginia, is a round dome, 69 feet (20 m) high.

Mounds in the Shapes of Animals

Some of the American mounds are very different from any of those in Europe. They were built in the shapes of giant animals.

In Wisconsin is a mound shaped like a giant bird with spread wings that are 600 feet (180 m) in length. What is the reason for these shapes? What could they have meant to the people who built them? Were they emblems or symbols of those people? Did they represent sacred or holy creatures? Were they simply works of art? We can only guess. Many of the mounds of America are as much of a mystery as the mounds of Europe.

The famous Great Serpent Mound in Ohio is in the shape of a writhing snake, about 1/4 of a mile (0.4 km) long.

3
THE STRANGE STANDING STONES

About 6,000 years ago, a little group of men dressed in clothing made of animal skins stood on a rocky hillside, peering about among the boulders of all shapes and sizes that lay there. The men quickly saw what they were looking for. It was a huge gray stone, twice as tall as any of the men and as thick as the whole length of a man's body. After talking among themselves for a few moments, the men left.

Several days later they returned with a number of other men. Some of them carried ropes made of braided leather, and others carried logs trimmed of their bark, and masses of dried straw. They twined ropes around the long gray stone they had selected. They spread a path of straw before it, and beyond the straw they placed the smooth logs in a row. Then, with some of them hauling on the ropes, they slid the stone over the slippery straw onto the logs. Pulling mightily, they began to drag it forward. It slid fairly easily over the logs, and as it passed over them, some of the men picked up the logs and hurried to place them in front of the stone again. In this way, the men hauled the stone several miles, to the place where they wanted to put it. It took them an entire day to get there.

Stone Giants

Some megaliths are truly enormous. The tallest one in all of Britain (which includes Scotland, England, and Wales) is 25 feet (7.7 m) high and 6 feet (1.8 m) wide. It stands in the middle of an old cemetery. In Brittany, on the French coast, is a megalith that is 31 feet (9.3 m) high and weighs 125 tons (112.5 metric tons). Also in Brittany is a single giant stone, the Grand Menhir Brisé, that was the largest ever set up anywhere in Europe. It now lies on the ground, broken into several pieces, probably by prehistoric people who intended to use the pieces for building dolmens; but when it was standing, it must have been almost 66 feet (20 m) tall and weighed 385 tons (350 metric tons).

The Grand Menhir Brisé

In this place, they had previously dug a pit in the ground. They tugged the stone forward until one end of it rested on the edge of the pit. They piled logs under the stone, slowly raising it. Pulling on the ropes they lifted the stone upward until it slipped into the pit. It stood there, on end, pointing up at the sky like a rough, knobby finger.

Events such as this took place many times during the New Stone Age. Many hundreds of single giant stones, set in place by prehistoric people, are still standing throughout Western Europe and in many parts of the world, including the United States.

Many standing stones in England are simply called the Long Stone, and in Scotland there's a megalith called by the cozy name Long Tom. However, many standing stones have special names of their own. These are not prehistoric names, as far as is known, but were probably given many hundreds of years ago by people who lived where the stones are standing. An 18-foot (5.6-m)-high stone on a Scottish isle is known as the Watch Stone. Were people supposed to watch the stone for some reason, or was the stone itself supposed to be watching for something? A thick, 6-foot (1.8-m) stone in Ireland is called the Stone of the Hounds. Whose hounds were they? Another Irish megalith is known as the Healing Stone, because it supposedly has a magical power to heal people. The gigantic fallen stone in Brittany, the Grand Menhir Brisé, is nicknamed the Fairy Stone, possibly because many of the Little People are supposed to live among the megaliths in Brittany. A stone in England is known as the Tingle Stone, because some people swear they feel a tingling sensation when they touch it. A pair of stones standing near each other in southern England are known as the Pipers. Were they once the site of musical events?

Legends of Ghosts, Blood, and Disaster

Many of the stones also have legends attached to them. A menhir in Ireland was said to have a container full of gold buried beneath it, guarded by a "terrible ghost." An English stone—one of those known as the Long Stone—is said to pull itself loose from where it stands and run around the field at midnight. Another English stone, known as the Whittlestone, is supposed to walk to a nearby well every midnight for a drink. A number of stones are said to bleed if they are jabbed with a needle. And throughout England, even as late as a century ago, there were stories that any attempt to move a standing stone would cause crops to wither, farm animals to sicken, and people to die.

It is barely possible that some of these legends actually provide hints of things that were done with these stones in prehistoric times. Perhaps the legends are the remains of descriptions that were passed down by word of mouth for thousands of years. Thus, legends of bleeding stones may reveal that the blood of sacrifices was once poured onto those stones. Legends of stones that drink water may indicate that water was once poured over them—perhaps an effort to cause rain to fall?

Curious Marks and Carvings

Most of the standing stones are plain, rough boulders, but a few have odd marks and carvings on them.

A number of European stones have round, cuplike holes gouged into them, formed of a number of circles, one inside another. Standing stones with similar ringed cuplike holes have been found in Georgia and Ohio. Some stones have long grooves running down their sides. No one knows why Stone Age people put these grooves and cup marks onto some of the stones they set up. Some archaeologists believe that the grooved lines were made to point toward particular stars for some reason. Some of the cup marks may be a symbol for the sun. If that is correct, the stones with such marks may have been used for worship of the sun in some way.

In Europe, prehistoric people set up standing stones from about 6,700 years ago to 3,500 years ago. The setting up of any of these huge stones must have been a titanic task for the people who did it. In most cases, the stones were apparently set up in very special places—for example, in Brittany, many stones were put near rivers, brooks, or wells. So most stones probably came from quite a distance away from where they were set up, and the only way to get a stone to where it was wanted was by having people pull it. Then

The Queen Stone and The Devil's Arrows

A 7-foot (2.10-m) stone called the Queen Stone, in England, has long, deep, straight grooves running down its length, on all sides. Three standing stones known as the Devil's Arrows, in another part of England, are also grooved in this way, and so is a stone in India.

The Devil's Arrows

the people faced the strenuous job of setting the stone upright. In the case of the Grand Menhir Brisé of Brittany, for example, it is known that it probably came from a rocky place about 9 miles (14.4 km) from where it was set up, and it has been estimated that it must have taken at least 1,000 people to drag it that far and get it upright.

Why Were Giant Stones Set Up?

The question is, what was the purpose of all these solitary giant stones? Why did the people of the New Stone Age spend such time and effort to set them up?

Were they grave markers or tombstones of great people? That doesn't seem likely, as no graves have been found under any of them. However, they could have been set up to honor people who were actually buried elsewhere.

Were they monuments of some great event, such as a victory in an important battle? Possibly. But there is no way to tell what that great event might have been.

Were they perhaps landmarks, to guide travelers on their way to somewhere? Some of them may well have been. One of the stones in England is known as the Way Stone, which seems to indicate that it was used to show the way to some place.

Some scientists who study the customs of people—anthropologists and archaeologists—believe that the standing stones may be symbols of a fertility religion that worshiped birth and growth, and that prehistoric people might have prayed to them for good crops and healthy farm animals. That is certainly possible. It's a known fact that some of these stones were actually being worshiped by people who lived near them less than a hundred years ago. Such worship might have been going on for thousands of years, left over from the time of the New Stone Age.

It is also possible that the stones marked meeting places, where tribes of prehistoric people might have come together to settle differences, to trade things with each other, or to arrange marriages between men and women of different tribes. They might have been markers, showing the boundaries between the lands of two tribes.

Some astronomers think that the stones might have been lined up with mountain peaks, hilltops, or other points on the horizon where the sun, the moon, a star, or a constellation may have risen or set on a particular day. Thus the stones may have been devices for marking a special holy day of some sort. This, too, is certainly possible, although it is almost impossible to tell at what point on the horizon a stone might be lined up—it could have been anywhere.

The Incredible Stone Rows of France

Near the seaside town of Carnac, in Brittany, stand more than 2,500 upright stones, ranging from 2 feet (60 cm) to about 13 feet (4 m) in height, arranged in long rows that stretch for nearly 2 miles (3.2 km). A great number of single megaliths, as well as megalithic tombs and a few structures, are also in the area. One of the single stones is the giant Fairy Stone, lying broken on the ground.

The rows of stones are in three groups. Some distance north of Carnac lies the Field of Menec—a name that, in the old language of Brittany, means the "Place of the Stones"—which has 1,099 stones

The Field of Menec

The Field of Kermario

arranged in 11 rows nearly 3/4 mile (1,207 m) long and 110 yards (100 m) wide. The rows taper slightly, so they are closer at the far end than at the beginning.

At the end of these rows is a space of about 474 yards (340 m), after which lies the Field of Kermario (which means the "Place of the Dead"), an arrangement of 982 stones in 10 rows a little less than 3/4 mile (1,207 m) long and 111 yards (101 m) wide. These rows also taper at the end.

After another space, of about 432 yards (393 m), is the Field of Kerlescan (the "Place of the Burning"), where 540 stones stand in 13 rows, covering an area 976 yards (880 m) long and 153 yards (139 m) wide.

Perhaps each standing stone was used for one of these purposes or for several of them. Perhaps they were used for different things in different places. But no one can tell for sure what their purpose actually was. The only thing we can be sure of is that they must have been very important to the prehistoric people of the New Stone Age, for they are found throughout the world.

The solitary standing stones left behind by the people of prehistoric times are indeed puzzling. But even more puzzling are the many places throughout the world where prehistoric people erected groups of standing stones, arranged in patterns. Many of these are circles, of as many as a dozen or more giant stones. Erecting such a group must have been tremendously difficult. But there is one particular place where the work that was done is so vast and imposing that it is truly mind-boggling. It is at Carnac, France, where prehistoric people set up thousands of huge stones in long straight rows, for a reason we can hardly guess at.

SUNRISE MARKERS? ECLIPSE PREDICTORS? PATHS TO STARS?

What were these incredible rows of giant stones for? A French scientist who studied the stone rows in the 1890s came to believe that they were a way of marking sunrises for sun worshipers. His idea was that people could have stood at one end of the pathway formed by two rows of stones and watched the sun rise between the last two stones at the end of the two rows. Of course, the sun does not always rise in the same place, so many rows were needed, and presumably that was why they had been built. This idea became accepted by many scientists. For several decades, the Field Museum of Natural History, in Chicago, had a lifesize diorama showing a prehistoric man, standing at the end of one of the "avenues" formed by two rows of stones at Carnac, his arms raised in worshipful greeting as he sees the sun rising between the last two stones, far in the distance.

Another scientist who studied the stone rows in the 1930s had a different idea. He believed that each row represented a clan (a group of related people within a tribe) of the prehistoric people of the Carnac area, and was a way for tribal leaders to keep records of all the people.

An English scientist who studied the stone rows in the 1960s became convinced they were part of a huge astronomical observatory, of which the giant Fairy Stone was the center. He believed that the Fairy Stone was meant to be lined up with a number of other standing stones that are visible in the distance, and used to chart the movements of the moon in order to be able to predict when eclipses would take place. However, other scientists have pointed out that Brittany is known to have been covered by thick forest 4,000 years ago, and it would not have been possible to see most of the other stones from the Fairy Stone, as it is now.

One of the newest ideas about the purpose of the rows at Carnac and other places is that they provided a steady path to follow toward the place on the horizon where a particular star rose. To take such a walk between two rows of giant stones, or along a single row, might have been an act of worship.

There are, of course, legends connected with the stone rows of Carnac, but they do not shed any light on what the rows might have been for. One legend says that the rows of stones were once rows of marching soldiers—an army that was turned to stone. Another says that the stone rows are the dwelling place of little dwarflike fairytale creatures known as Kerions. These sound like stories that might have been made up to try to explain the stones to children.

Other Stone Rows and Arrangements

There are a great many rows of large standing stones in England, Scotland, and Ireland; and in the Netherlands, where large stones are scarce, the remains of rows of Stone Age wooden posts have been found. There is said to be an arrangement of standing stones much like those at Carnac in the highlands of Tibet, thousands of miles away. They consist of 18 rows of huge stones, running east and west, with a circle of stones at the western edge of each one. There are some rows of standing stones in the Arab Republic of Yemen, which run toward a small circle of stones. There is no way of telling whether these rows were used in the same way as the stone avenues of Carnac. All these rows are simply another of the great mysteries left over from long ago.

Another kind of arrangement of stones has been found in southern Egypt in what is called the Eastern Desert, a part of the Sahara. This arrangement is definitely linked to a sky event, and it is the oldest-known such megalithic structure in the world—at least 6,000 years old, and possibly as much as 6,500 years old. Even though it is far older than the structures of Carnac, a great deal more is known about its purpose.

Called Nabta, it was constructed by wandering cattle herders at the edge of a lake that then covered what is now desert. There, rituals may have been held in connection with the summer solstice, which would have been an important time for the herdsmen, because it marked the beginning of heavy rains that turned the region green, providing food for the cattle.

About 4,800 years ago, due to a shift in weather patterns, the heavy rains stopped falling in the Nabta area, and the lake dried up.

Nabta

Nabta spreads over an area 1.8 miles (2.8 km) by about 3/4 mile (1,207 km). It consists of several kinds of structures. One is formed of five lines of huge stone slabs, about 9 feet (2.7 m) high, some lying flat and some standing. Another consists of 30 oval pits, each covered with 40 to 50 large rocks that weigh from 200 to 300 pounds (90–135 kg) each. A third is a 12-foot (3.6-m)-wide circle of 18-inch (45-cm) stone slabs, most lying flat, but with four pairs of upright slabs, arranged around the edge of the circle.

Two pairs of these are set directly across from each other, and are aligned in a north-south direction. The other two pair are also directly across from each other, and are set up so that a person standing behind one of

the pairs on the morning of the summer solstice would have been looking straight toward the sunrise. About three weeks before and three weeks after the solstice, the sun would have been at its highest position in the sky over the circle, and at exactly noon the standing stones would not have cast any shadow. It seems likely that this stone circle may have been used for holding ceremonies at noon around the time of the summer solstice.

The cattle herding people abandoned their stone structure and moved somewhere else. Some scientists believe that these people, with their knowledge of erecting stones and using them to mark events in the sky, may have played a part in helping to create the civilization of ancient Egypt.

Who Were the "Little People?"

Legends of the Little People—Fairy Folk—still cling to the Fairy Stone (also known as the Grand Menhir Brisé) of Carnac, the rows of standing stones, and many of the mounds and megaliths of the British Isles. Why should fairies be associated with so many standing stones and structures built by the New Stone Age people?

There have been some scientists who believed that perhaps it was because the New Stone Age people actually *were* the Little People!

Most New Stone Age people of France and the British Isles certainly were rather small, many no bigger than a nine- or ten-year-old child of today. France and Britain were invaded by people from other parts of Europe in the centuries following the end of the Stone Age, and some of those people may have been a good deal bigger. It's possible that the descendents of the people who built the megalithic structures hid from the big invaders, and became regarded with rather awed curiosity. At times they might have held ceremonies and rituals at the structures their ancestors had built, and to the tall newcomers it could have seemed as if the furtive little people were performing spooky rites of magic at the mysterious earth mounds and strange rings of giant stones. Legends would have begun about the little people and their magical ways. And legends have a way of lasting for thousands of years.

Many scientists deny that things could have happened that way. But a few have believed that it's a logical explanation for why there are so many legends that associate fairies—the Little People—with the mounds and megalithic structures of prehistoric times.

4
STONEHENGE—THE PUZZLE ON THE PLAIN

On the Isle of Britain a number of structures, known as henges, remain from prehistoric times. Similar structures, called by different names, have also been found in Ireland, Germany, and other countries. A henge was made by people digging a circular ditch around a flat area of ground, and piling up the earth that came out of the ditch into a thick low wall all around the ditch. The area enclosed by the ditch and wall might be as much as several hundred yards (meters) wide.

CONSTRUCTING A HENGE

To make such a structure, prehistoric people had to be able to measure out a perfect circle for the ditch and wall, so we know they must have had some knowledge of mathematics. They probably measured the circle by pounding a stake into the ground, tying a long leather rope to it, then having someone walk around the stake with the rope stretched out to its full length. This would have caused the person to walk in a perfect circle, with the stake at the

Stonehenge

The most famous of all prehistoric henges is Stonehenge, which stands on a rolling plain in the south of England. It is basically a circle formed of huge gray stones with more stones inside it in a horseshoe-shape, standing in the center of a circle of flat ground surrounded by earthen walls and a ditch. The main stones are 13 feet (4 m) high, and are cut roughly into rectangles. Today, many of the stones are gone, having been carried off in past centuries and used for building bridges, churches, and other things. Many of the others have toppled over and now lie flat on the ground. But enough are left to show that Stonehenge was once a truly grand and awesome structure.

center. As the person holding the rope walked, a pebble might have been put down, or a mark made in the earth, at every few steps. Thus, when the walkaround was finished, there would have been a perfect circle of pebbles or marks, to be followed when people started digging.

However, while most henges are perfect circles, not all are. Some are flattened circles, like a pie with one side straight instead of curved. Some are ellipses, which is a shape somewhat like the outline of a fat football. Some are ovals. It does not seem as if the non-circular shapes were just the result of sloppy measuring; it appears as if they were deliberately made that way. But why, is a mystery.

Many henges consisted of nothing more than a wall and ditch, but others were more complicated. Patterns of tall standing stones or wooden posts were sometimes set up inside the walls. Long walkways, or "avenues," were sometimes built leading to them. Single standing stones were placed here and there. But the reasons for this, like the reason for the different shapes of henges, are completely unknown to us now.

A Choice of Sacred Ground

It is known that Stonehenge was built and rebuilt over a period of just about 2,000 years, by different groups of people, and that its design was changed several times. The place the prehistoric people chose to build Stonehenge was a region where many structures had already been built. There were long barrows nearby, each holding the bones of many people, hundreds of years old before Stonehenge was begun.

Less than a mile from where Stonehenge was built is a strange structure known as the Cursus, which means "track." It consists of two low earthen walls with ditches on their outer sides, about 350 feet (105 m) apart, stretched side by side for a distance of 2 miles (3.2 km). At one end of the walls is a long barrow; at the other end the walls are joined together with an oblong curve. This structure was probably there before Stonehenge was built. There are remains of 50 similar structures in Britain, but none anywhere else. Some archaeologists think that these strange "tracks" may have been used for processions of some sort.

A short distance from Stonehenge, in what is now the parking lot, there had been a little row of three stout wooden posts, made from pine trees, that were set in the ground as much as 10,000 years ago, and were probably long gone before work on Stonehenge was begun. And about 2 miles from the site of Stonehenge was an ancient henge, a circular ditch and wall that may have been a dwelling place for prehistoric people. So it seems as if the area where Stonehenge was built might have been regarded as rather special by prehistoric people, perhaps a sacred region where the dead had been buried and structures built for many generations.

The Beginning of Stonehenge

The first form of Stonehenge was begun about 5,000 years ago. After marking out their circle, the makers of the first Stonehenge followed the marks and dug out a deep circular ditch. From the earth dug out of the ditch they built a 6-foot (1.8-m)-high, 320-foot (96-m)-wide wall all around the inner side of the ditch, and a much smaller wall around the outside. The soil where Stonehenge was built lies atop a deep layer of soft chalk, so the walls must have been a glaring white. There was a fairly broad opening, or entrance, in the section of walls facing northeast, and a narrower entrance in the south. Some time after finishing this, the builders dug a circle of 56 evenly-spaced, 3-foot (1-m)-deep holes just inside the inner wall.

The first Stonehenge had no circles of giant stones. It was simply a structure made of earth. But constructing it must have been fairly difficult for people with nothing to work with but deer antlers for picks, hip bones of wild oxen for shovels, and stone axes. Archaeologists can tell there weren't many people living in the region, so it must have taken them a long time to make such a structure. Stonehenge must have been very important to them, but the reason is a mystery for us today.

What Was It For?

Some facts are known. The 56 holes forming the circle inside the wall were filled in with chalk and broken stones soon after they were dug. But sometime later, this rubble was removed, and at least 25 of the holes were filled with the ashes of burned human bones as well as ax heads and bone ornaments for clothing. Thus the holes had been turned into graves. Ashes of the bones of about thirty more people, who were buried about this time, have also been found in various parts of the circle. These were not all buried at the same time, but over a period of many years. This certainly makes it seem as if Stonehenge might have been a kind of cemetery or huge burial place, like the barrows around it.

However, there was more to the first Stonehenge than just burials. The people who built it took great care to see that it could be used to watch something that happened in the sky on a certain day each year. Today, a person who stands in the center of the circle at sunrise on the first day of summer (June 21, the summer solstice) and looks through the entrance in the wall will see the sun rise just left of the large megalith that now stands there and quickly move upward until it appears to be perched on the stone's peak. It seems that the opening in the wall was made there especially so that sunrise could be seen from inside the circle. This suggests that Stonehenge might have been a kind of calendar, for keeping track of the summer solstice every year. It might have been a great temple, of a religion that worshiped the sun. Perhaps, like Newgrange, Stonehenge linked the dead people buried inside its wall with the sunrise.

A Stone-Age Observatory

There have been astronomers who believed Stonehenge was something a great deal more complicated than that. They figured out that by using the circle of 56 holes inside Stonehenge's circular wall, it could have been possible to keep track of the time between eclipses of the sun and moon, and thus be able to tell when the next one was coming. Prehistoric people would have had a good reason for wanting to be able to do this. Primitive people have

Some of the many stages in the evolution of Stonehenge

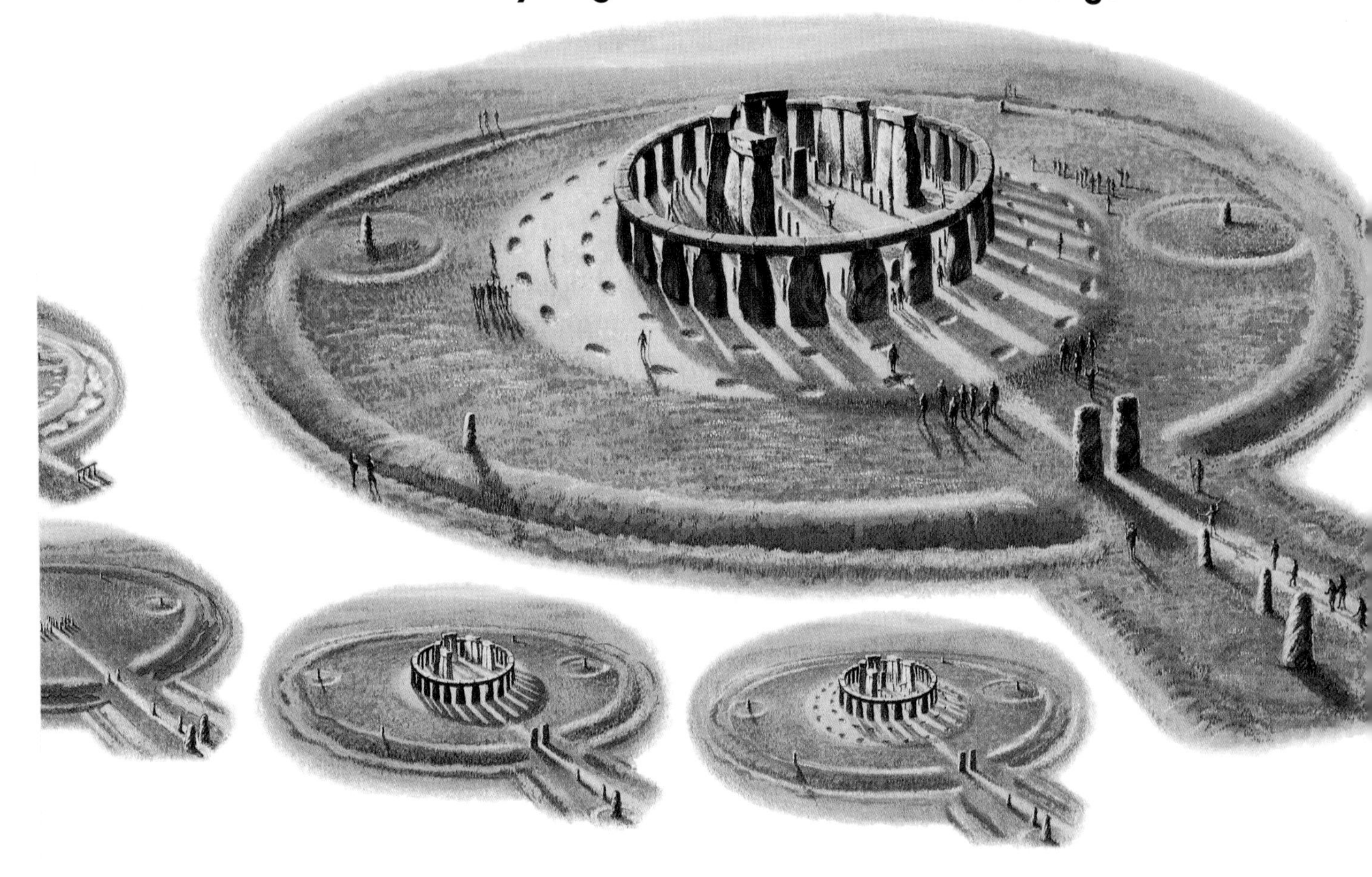

always been terrified of eclipses, because when one occurred, it seemed as if the world were coming to an end. For most primitive people eclipses came as a sudden unpleasant surprise, so if the prehistoric people of the Stonehenge region could have known an eclipse was coming, they might have felt this gave them an advantage—they could prepare a mighty religious ritual to help prevent the world from ending.

However, to use the holes in such a way would have taken a special method of counting, based on a thorough knowledge of the movement of the sun and moon. It would have meant that the circle of holes was being used as a kind of primitive computer, more than 5,000 years ago. Did the prehistoric people of that one

Stonehenge sarsens

This ring of upright stones and lintels would have resembled the ring of wooden posts and wooden lintels that had once stood in the circle of 56 holes, 400 years before. Did the people who put up the stones know this? Could the stones and the wooden poles have served exactly the same purpose?

Strange Ideas About Stonehenge

For many centuries, people have tried to figure out how Stonehenge was built, and what it might have been used for. Some of their ideas have been strange and weird.

One of the oldest ideas, going back nearly a thousand years, was that Stonehenge was put up by the great magician Merlin, who was the wizard of the famous King Arthur.

According to this legend, Stonehenge had originally been built in Ireland, by giants, and was known as the Giants Dance. When the English King Aurelius Ambrosius, Arthur's father, wanted to erect a great monument to commemorate a battle, Merlin suggested using the Giants Dance. He went to Ireland, took all the stones down by means of magic, and then magically reassembled them in England.

So, according to this legend, Stonehenge wasn't even built by humans; it was set up where it is now, as if by magic.

In modern times, the ideas have gotten even stranger. A large number of people don't believe that Stonehenge could possibly have been built by prehistoric humans. They believe it must have been built by aliens from outer space.

However, archaeologists and other scientists have found plenty of evidence that Stonehenge was indeed built by people of the New Stone Age, who were clever and skillful enough to figure out how to move huge megaliths and arrange them into rings, rows, and dolmens. We know who built Stonehenge and how they did it. What we still don't know is why.

The stones that formed the ring and horseshoe were probably brought to Stonehenge from a rocky region about 20 miles (32 km) away. This certainly must have been easier than bringing the bluestones, but even so it was still a gigantic job, for some of these giant stones weigh as much as 40 tons (36 metric tons).

Shaping the Stones

To begin with, the stones were all "trimmed" to be given a smoother, more even shape, with the tops squared off and the sides straightened. This was done by chiseling long straight cuts into the stone with sharp-edged stone axes. The cut was then packed with dry leaves and twigs, which were set afire. When the fire was blazing well, cold water was quickly poured onto it, and large heavy chunks of rock were instantly dropped onto the cut line. Generally, this would fracture the stone, causing it to crack in a straight line following the cut, and break off. This was a slow process that had to be done to each stone several times. It probably took many months to trim them all.

The trimming was done at the place where the stones were found, and when each stone was satisfactorily squared off, it had to be hauled away to Stonehenge by huge crews of men, and perhaps women, too, over a "road" of peeled logs. When a stone finally got to Stonehenge, it was placed at the edge of a pit that had been dug for it, and tugged upright into the pit with ropes. To lay the lintel stones onto the upright ones, scaffolding made of logs was ponderously put together beneath each lintel, slowly raising it to the top of the standing stones. Then it was pulled into place with ropes. The lintels fit well and didn't slide off, because a bump had been chiseled on top of each standing stone that fit exactly into a shallow hole made at each end of the lintel. This not only shows how skillful the prehistoric people were at carving stone, but also how well they were able to measure things.

This work of putting the ring and horseshoe of stones into place had been a tremendous undertaking. It has been estimated that if there were 500 people working every day, it would have taken them 34 years to do what was done.

Durrington Walls

While all the building and rebuilding of Stonehenge was going on, another henge—an enormous one—was being built nearby, about 2 miles (3.2 km) from Stonehenge. The remains of this henge are known today as Durrington Walls. When it was first built, it consisted of a circular earth wall and ditch, enclosing an area about 500 yards (450 m) wide. Traces of circles of wooden posts have been found inside the remains of the wall, and these may have been the walls of large houses or other buildings. This huge henge may have been a sort of enclosed village. Because it was so close, archaeologists wonder if it may have had some connection to Stonehenge.

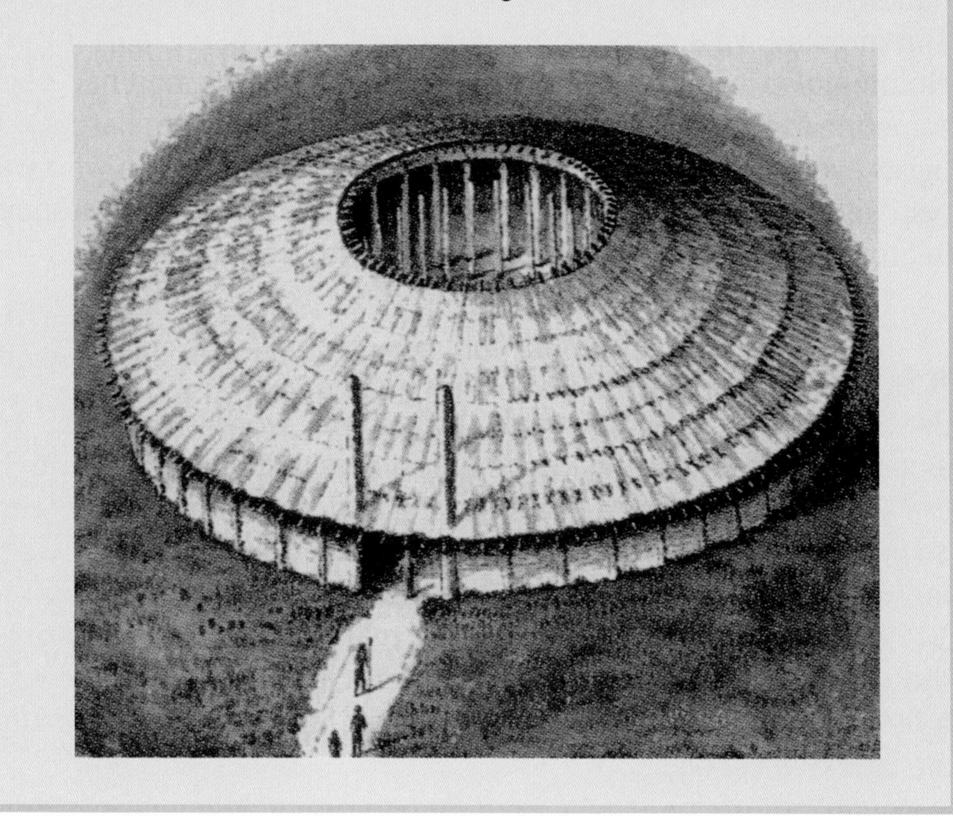

Stone-Age Totem Poles?

When a parking lot was being constructed for visitors to Stonehenge, workers discovered the remains of three large, round holes, about 260 feet (80 m) away from the edge of Stonehenge. They were about 3 feet (1 m) deep and 6 feet (2 m) wide. Archaeologists found that they had contained wooden poles that had probably been set up around 10,000 years ago. This was 5,000 years before Stonehenge was even begun, so they weren't part of Stonehenge. What could they have been for?

Most archaeologists think they could have been totem poles, like the totem poles put up by certain Native American tribes of North America. They were probably thick, tall tree trunks that had all the bark peeled off them and were then carved with designs and figures that had a meaning for the Stone Age people who lived in that time and place. Unfortunately, we can never know what those carvings might have looked like.

outside of the wall. Why? Did the people who began the digging just decide to do it that way on a whim, or was there some reason? There is no answer.

And so Stonehenge remains one of the greatest of the puzzles left over from the prehistoric world. Was it a great temple of a religion that had something to do with death and the sun? Was it indeed an astronomical observatory, for studying the movement of the sun and moon and computing the occurrence of eclipses? Some people firmly believe it was one of these things, but no one really knows for sure.

5
CIRCLES OF STONE AND WOOD

The creation of giant circles of huge stones, and sometimes of thick poles of wood, seems to have played a very important part in the lives of prehistoric people. There are some 900 stone circles standing in the British Isles alone, and scores more are scattered throughout Europe, from France to Romania. Circles of stones have also been found in parts of the United States, India, Africa, on islands in the Mediterranean Sea, and in a remote valley in Tibet. Some of them stand within henges, as Stonehenge does; others are built around other structures, such as mounds; but most simply stand by themselves.

A Great Temple?

The largest of all stone circles known is Avebury, in England, not far from Stonehenge. Today, several roads cross through it and a little town lies right on it. So many of Avebury's stones are missing that it is impossible to tell if Avebury could ever have been used as any kind of astronomical observatory, as Stonehenge and other stone

Avebury, the World's Largest Stone Circle

Four thousand years ago, Avebury consisted of an enormous circle of 100 standing stones, more than 400 yards (360 m) across, surrounded by a ditch and a wall of earth. Within the circle of stones were two smaller stone circles, each about 114 yards (102 m) wide. A 1.5-mile (2.4-km)-long pathway, lined on each side with 12-foot (3.6-m) standing stones, wound up to the main stone circle.

Avebury was not built in the same way as Stonehenge. Its two stone circles were constructed first, probably 4,600 years ago. The stones came from the same place as the stones that form the horseshoe and inner circle at Stonehenge. After the circles were completed, the huge ditch and wall that encircle Avebury were begun. The ditch was 11 yards (10 m) deep—and enough chalky soil was taken out of it to build a wall 20 feet (6 m) high and 33 yards (30 m) wide.

In one of the two small rings of stone, three huge stones were set up touching one another, to form three sides of a rectangle. Only one of the stones is still standing. A short distance outside Avebury another of these structures was built. They are known as Coves, and what they were for is a mystery. However, they were built very much like the entrances to many of the long mounds that are around Avebury, so archaeologists believe they may have been used for rituals involving dead people.

Stanton Drew

About 30 miles (48 km) from Avebury, in a little valley ringed with rolling hills, is a smaller version of Avebury. It consists of a large circle of stones, about 49 yards (113.5 m) wide, with a short avenue leading into it, and two ellipses of standing stones, one a short distance northeast of the big circle and one to the southwest. The circle to the northeast also has a short avenue leading into it. Some distance from the three circles is a cove of three stones, like the one at Avebury. All this was built about 4,500 years ago, by people who apparently had the same beliefs as those who built Avebury. Perhaps if Avebury was like a great cathedral, this smaller construction, now called Stanton Drew, was like a country church.

circles might have been. But because of its huge size and grandeur, most experts think that it was most probably a kind of great temple, which apparently was in use for a good thousand years after its building was finished, where prehistoric people went for special rituals and services that made them feel confident and inspired—just as people go to churches and temples today.

STONE CIRCLES IN FRANCE

On a tiny isle close to the coast of Brittany, in France, are two stone circles that were apparently set up to form a kind of figure-8. This was done about 4,500 years ago. The water has risen since then, and the circles are now often under water, so many of the stones have been dislodged. But a number of interesting things have been found—bits of pottery, stone tools, oxen teeth, stone axes. It seems as if these things may have been "offerings" of some sort. Archaeologists have also found the remains of a number of fires within the circles, and believe that ceremonies might have been held there, involving several hundred people. Some of the stones apparently were lined up to mark the rising and setting of the moon on the night of Midwinter, and that is probably when the ceremonies were held. One of the stones has nine cupmarks on it, another has marks that may represent a plow, two others have axes carved into them, and one of these also has some strange marks that look a bit like the letter P. These two stone circles may have been a very important place for the New Stone Age people who lived in the area.

CIRCLES OF DANCING STONES

In southernmost England stands a ring of 19 stones about 26 yards (23.4 m) wide, known as the Merry Maidens. According to legend, the stones were once girls who were turned into stones because they were dancing when they shouldn't have been. This circle also has a much older name, in another language, which is the Stone Dance. About 40 miles (64 km) away is a circle of 12 stones known as the Trippet Stones, which are also supposed to be girls turned to stone for dancing.

Long Meg and Her Daughters

Another famous British stone circle is known as Long Meg and Her Daughters. This is a large ring, flattened on one side, but over 120 yards (109.4 m) across. It consists of 60 short, stout boulders, with a slim, 12-foot (3.6-m)-tall reddish stone standing about 25 yards (22.5 m) outside the ring. The tall stone is Long Meg, and the 60 short stones are the daughters.

Like Stonehenge, Long Meg and Her Daughters is lined up to show a movement of the sun; in this case it is a sunset rather than a sunrise. A person standing in the center of the ring on the evening of Midwinter Day will see the sun go down directly behind Long Meg.

On the side of Long Meg that faces the circle, there are carvings. One is a cup-and-ring with a groove running out of it, one is a spiral, another is a group of small circles, one inside another, with two half-circles over them. There are also some faint cup marks. There is no way to tell when these carvings were made or what they mean. However, because carvings such as these are often found on tombs, many archaeologists believe they symbolize life, death, and the sun. One legend has it that Long Meg and Her Daughters were witches, who were turned to stone for their wickedness. Another legend says that if a piece of Long Meg is chipped off, the stone will bleed in that place.

In still another part of southern England are two rings of stones, side by side, known as the Grey Wethers, and it is said the stones dance at sunrise, by slowly spinning in their holes. The Athgreany circle, in Ireland, is also known as the Pipers Stones, which might indicate that music was once played there, and legend says that the stones were men who were turned to stone for doing an ancient pagan dance. A legend of another stone circle in England tells that at midnight the stones turn into men who join hands and dance. Many archaeologists believe that such names and legends, which connect stone circles with dancing, may actually reach back to prehistoric times, when people might have danced in the stone circles as part of a religious ceremony.

Circles of Sacrifice

Some of the legends of stone circles are dark and bloody. Athgreany Circle, in Ireland, stands in a meadow that has the old, old name of the Sun Field, and legends hint that human sacrifices were made there to the sun in prehistoric times. In the circle known as the Druid's Circle, in Wales, one of the standing stones has a slight ledge projecting from it, on which, according to legend, were placed the bodies of sacrificed children.

There actually is possible evidence of human sacrifice at the Druid's Circle. This circle consists of a low, circular wall of earth and stones, about 30 yards (27 m) wide, inside of which is a ring of 30 stones, each about 5 to 6 feet (1.5-1.8 m) long. Only 12 are still standing upright. Beneath a little group of rocks at the center of the circle were found the burned bones of a child, about eleven years old. The bones of another child, of the same age, were found buried nearby. Many archaeologists think these children were sacrifices.

Some stone circles that very much resemble Stonehenge have been found in parts of the world far from England. A British explorer found a great stone circle in the desert of Saudi Arabia. He described it as a number of huge stones standing on end, with other great stones lying across their tops like the lintels of Stonehenge. A similar circle of stones was found in the North African country of Libya. And in the Central African nation of Kenya there is a circle of 19 big volcanic stones that are lined up

Callanish—The Stonehenge of the North

The stone circle called Callanish, which stands on an island off the coast of Scotland, is known as "the Stonehenge of the North." It consists of a 15-foot (4.75-m) megalith inside a circle of 13 smaller megaliths. The circle is flattened on one side, and is about 12 yards (10.8 m) wide. An avenue formed by two rows of

standing stones stretches away from the north side of the circle, and three short rows of stones lead away from the east, west, and south. It may be that these rows were going to be made into avenues too, but were never finished. Perhaps the builders of Callanish planned to have ceremonial processions march into the circle using different avenues at different times of the year.

Some astronomers feel they have found evidence indicating that Callanish could have been used as a calendar. The 13 stones forming the ring consist of 12 large stones and one smaller one. The 12 large stones could have represented the 12 months of what is called the lunar (moon) year, which has only 354 days, and the small stone could have been used to count the additional days forming an actual year of 365 days.

There is a rather weird legend about Callanish. It was said that on sunrise of the first day of summer, the call of a cuckoo was heard, and then a shining "something" came walking up the avenue toward the ring. This sounds as if Callanish was regarded as a holy place, and stories tell of people worshiping there since prehistoric times, until just a few hundred years ago.

with the rising and setting of certain stars. It was erected 2,300 years ago, by people who were still living in the Stone Age, but it is still used as a calendar by people living near it today.

It is clear that all around the world, communities of Stone Age people hundreds and thousands of miles from one another erected great circles of stone that were of tremendous importance to them. Perhaps their reasons for doing this were all much the same.

Circles of Wood

Most archaeologists believe that before New Stone Age people built any circles of stone, they put up circles of wooden posts made from tree trunks, as was done at Stonehenge. Remains of such circles, dating from the New Stone Age, have been found in the British Isles and other places. Basically, they are just circles of holes in the ground, in which there are traces of ancient rotted wood that once were poles.

From Wooden Building to Stone Circle

It seems as if many stone circles made by Stone Age people may actually have been copies of wood circles that were built first. The wooden posts were simply replaced by stones. Some 17 miles (27

Woodhenge

The best-known wooden circle is only 2 miles (3 km) from Stonehenge, and has been named Woodhenge. It dates from at least 4,000 years ago, and consists of a henge—a low earth wall, a shallow ditch, and a roundish flat area—in which are six egg-shaped circles of holes, one inside another. Originally, the holes were filled with wooden posts.

Woodhenge was built just outside the huge henge known as Durrington Walls, and at just about the same time, so archaeologists wonder if there was some connection between the two. In 1981 a mathematician made a careful study of Woodhenge and determined that the holes for the posts were dug without any attempt to make the spaces between them even, and without any particular plan or design. Many archaeologists think the posts held up a domed roof, so perhaps Woodhenge was simply a building of some

sort, sitting inside a wall. But a number of scientists believe that Woodhenge was not a building at all, but was actually a structure of many posts arranged so that it was possible to view certain sunrises between pairs of them.

There is something very disturbing about Woodhenge. Buried within the center ring was the skeleton of a child, about three years old. It was facing in the direction of sunrise on the morning of summer solstice, and its skull was split open as if by the single blow of a stone ax. Most archaeologists regard this as a clear example of human sacrifice. What was so important about this wooden structure that it required a sacrifice? Could Woodhenge have been a temple or a holy place for prehistoric people?

Perhaps it is significant that buried in some of the post holes at Woodhenge were axes made of chalk. Such axes couldn't have been used to chop anything, for they would have crumbled to bits at the first blow. They must have been just symbols of axes, or symbols for something that axes might have represented. Were axes sacred or holy to the people who erected Woodhenge? Is this why the little girl was killed with an ax?

km) from Woodhenge, at the top of a hill, are the remains of just such a structure, which is known as the Sanctuary.

Another Sacrifice?

Like Woodhenge, there is a darkness shrouding the Sanctuary. Beneath where the single standing stone had been, at its very center, was found the skeleton of a fourteen- or fifteen-year-old young person, probably a girl. She had been buried facing toward the rising sun, with her hands covering her face. Was this, too, a sacrifice? There were no marks of violence on the skeleton, but she could have been killed in a way that wouldn't have left any. Was this young girl deliberately killed, and buried in the center of the Sanctuary with a megalith placed on top of her, in order to give the stones "power," or to become the Sanctuary's guardian spirit?

The remains of several other prehistoric wood structures have been found in England and nearby parts of Europe. One, near the town of Arminghall, England, had been shaped like a horseshoe, open at one end. The horseshoe was formed of eight posts, each about 3 feet (1 m) thick, inside a wide circular wall of earth. A number of wood structures, in both England and the Netherlands, had several circles of posts, one inside another, like Woodhenge, but mounds of earth had been built over them.

Wood Circles in America

There are also woodhenges in America. Two have been found at Cahokia, Illinois, where Monks Mound stands, which was a center of the Native American Mississippian culture, from 1,300 to about 500 years ago. The largest, which is about a half-mile west of Monks Mound, was a ring of 48 posts, 410 feet (123 m) wide, with a single post in the middle. The posts were about as thick as a modern telephone pole, and probably stood about 30 feet (9 m) high. Apparently, a person standing in front of the center pole could look toward certain other poles and see the sun rise behind them on the mornings of the summer and winter solstices. So the American woodhenge, like some of the stone circles of Europe, might have been a kind of calendar or observatory for following the movement of the sun. But unlike the English woodhenge and some of the stone circles, there is no evidence of any human sacrifice at the American woodhenge.

The remains of what might have been similar woodhenges have also been found in Kansas, and there is evidence of a 3,000-year-old one in Louisiana. The remains of woodhenges might exist in many places of the world, but they would be extremely hard to find. The holes are surely filled in and covered over with plant life, so a person could walk right over some of them without noticing and without ever knowing that once, ages ago in that very spot, prehis-

The Sanctuary

When it was first built, about 5,000 years ago, the Sanctuary consisted of an outer ring of 12 posts, about 32 feet (9.6 m) wide, with an inner ring of eight taller posts, 16 feet (4.8 m) wide. The posts were made from trunks of oak trees from a nearby wood. Archaeologists feel that these circles of posts were probably the walls of a building with a dome-shaped roof. They are also fairly sure that the building was a place where bodies were stored until the flesh had rotted off them and the skeletons could be taken to a long barrow for burial.

About 200 years later, the Sanctuary building was replaced with something different. An 80-foot (24-m)-wide circle of posts forming a kind of fence was put up, and in the middle of it was a 13-foot (4-m)-wide circle of posts with a single post in the center. This was probably a small building, still used as a place to store bodies. But not long after this construction was finished, another change was made. The round fence of poles was made much smaller, only 48 feet (14 m) wide, and the circle of posts forming the walls of the building in the middle was replaced with much thicker posts, making the building much sturdier. In the center of this circle was a single thick post.

Then, about 4,300 years ago, 600 years after it was begun, all the wooden posts were replaced with standing stones. The Sanctuary had become a stone copy of what it had looked like when it was made of wooden posts. It stood that way for thousands of years, but in 1724 the stones were all broken up and used as building material.

toric people might have held great ceremonies and rituals that were a vitally important part of their life.

Stonehenge, Woodhenge, Monks Mound, Carnac, Nabta—throughout the world stand the remains of these strange circles, rows, dolmens, and mounds. They are often thousands of miles apart, and it is obvious that the prehistoric people who built them could never have encountered one another. Yet, from Europe to Africa to Asia to the Americas, many of these ancient monuments are strangely similar. It seems plain that the people of the New Stone Age, wherever they lived, all thought in much the same way. They used stone and earth to make great structures that had deep significance for them. But we can never really know exactly what these things meant to those people of that time long ago.

WHY CIRCLES?

Why were so many of the stone and wood structures made by prehistoric people in the shape of circles? Why are there no squares, or rectangles, or triangles?

The circle had a very special importance for prehistoric people. There were two circles that played a big part in their lives—the sun and the full moon. They didn't know what the sun was, of course, but they knew that it gave them warmth and had something to do with making plants grow. They probably thought it was a supernatural object, perhaps even a god. A glowing full moon was probably also regarded as a supernatural thing.

There are many circles in nature that ancient people associated with the sun and moon. The center of a daisy—from "day's eye," a name for the sun—is a circle, and so is the center of sunflowers. The round glossy-white berry of the mistletoe plant looks like a little moon, and it is known that ancient people collected them for magical rituals.

There is also another natural circle, which suddenly appears from time to time as if by magic. This is the circle of mushrooms known since ancient times as a Fairy Ring. A Fairy Ring happens because some mushrooms grow from threadlike fibers that spread out in an almost perfect circle underground. A Fairy Ring can shoot up overnight, and such an event must have seemed like magic to prehistoric people.

The stone circles that prehistoric people built may have represented the sun or moon. A circle may have been thought to have some magical power.

FURTHER RESOURCES

FURTHER READING

Able, Harriet S. *Stonehenge*. Parsippany, NJ: Silver Burdett, 1987.

Chippendale, Christopher. *Stonehenge Complete*. Ithaca, NY: Cornell University Press, 1993.

Martin, Ana. *Prehistoric Stone Monuments*. Danbury, CT: Children's Press, 1993.

Masters, Anthony. *Serpent Mound*. New York: Simon and Schuster, 1996.

Roop, Peter and Connie. *Stonehenge: Opposing Viewpoints*. San Diego, CA: Greenhaven, 1989.

Silverburg, Robert. *The Mound Builders*. Athens, OH: Ohio University Press, 1986.

INTERNET RESOURCES

The Internet is rapidly evolving and these sites may no longer be valid. A keyword search is the best way to find the latest, up-to-date information on almost any topic.

Mystic Places: Stonehenge—Discovery Channel Canada visits this massive and mysterious construction.
http://exn.ca/mysticplaces/stonehenge.cfm

This Universiy of Colorado at Boulder Web site gives more information on Nabta, the ancient Egyptian site.
http://www.eurekalert.org/releases/ucob-oastmdiept.html

The Ohio Historical Society provides a directory of historic sites and museums. The address listed is for the Serpent Mound and includes directions, should you want to visit.
http://www.oplin.lib.oh.us/products/site/sites/southwest/serpm.html

INDEX

Page numbers in *italics* refer to illustrations.